HARRY S.
TRUMAN

PRESIDENTIAL ✦ LEADERS

HARRY S. TRUMAN

CAROLINE EVENSEN LAZO

LERNER PUBLICATIONS COMPANY / MINNEAPOLIS

For Stephanie, Peter, and Chip

The author would like to thank the staff of the Harry S. Truman Library and Museum of Independence, Missouri, for their assistance with this book.

Lerner Publications Company
A division of Lerner Publishing Group
241 First Avenue North
Minneapolis, MN 55401 U.S.A.

Website address: www.lernerbooks.com

Library of Congress Cataloging-in-Publication Data

Lazo, Caroline Evensen.
    Harry S. Truman / by Caroline Evensen Lazo.
        p.   cm. — (Presidential leaders series)
    Includes bibliographical references and index.
    Summary: Discusses the private life and political career of Harry S. Truman, who served as president from 1945 to 1953.
    ISBN: 0–8225–0096–5 (lib. bdg. : alk. paper)
    1. Truman, Harry S, 1884–1972—Juvenile literature. 2. Presidents—United States—Biography—Juvenile literature. [1. Truman, Harry S, 1884–1972. 2. Presidents.] I. Title.
II. Series.
E814 .L39 2003
973.918'092—dc21   2001006411

Manufactured in the United States of America
1 2 3 4 5 6 – JR – 08 07 06 05 04 03

CONTENTS

———————— ✧ ————————

After only weeks of serving as vice president, Harry S. Truman suddenly found himself with the most powerful job in the world.

CHAPTER ONE

WHEN LIGHTNING STRUCK

A good president has to be a man—or as of course will come in time, a woman—who works for the people in a way that makes a great impression on the period in which he lives.

—Harry S. Truman

Shortly before five o'clock on the evening of April 12, 1945, Vice President Harry S. Truman arrived at the private office of Speaker of the House Sam Rayburn. He was looking forward to an evening of relaxing with friends after a long afternoon of listening to speeches in the Senate. But on his arrival, Truman learned that he had just received a call from the White House. It had come from Steve Early, President Roosevelt's press secretary. When Truman returned the call, Early told the vice president to come to the White House as "quickly and quietly" as possible.

President Roosevelt (left) was apparently in ill health during this 1945 press conference with Vice President Truman (right). The president died later that year in Warm Springs, Georgia.

Truman left Rayburn's office immediately—running through the basement corridors of the Capitol and into his chauffeured limousine. He moved so fast that he left behind the Secret Service agents charged with guarding his safety. Truman knew President Roosevelt had been in ill health for some time. But he did not want to think about what might have happened. "I thought I was going down there to meet the President," he later said. "I didn't allow myself to think anything else."

When Truman arrived at the White House, he was escorted by elevator to First Lady Eleanor Roosevelt's private quarters on the second floor. Mrs. Roosevelt walked over to him and placed her arm across his shoulders. "Harry," she said, "the President is dead."

Truman was stunned. For a moment, he was speechless. Finally he asked Mrs. Roosevelt, "Is there anything I can do for you?"

With her characteristic thoughtfulness, she replied, "Is there anything we can do for *you?* For you are the one in trouble now."

Harry S. Truman was now president of the United States.

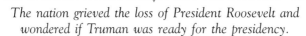

The nation grieved the loss of President Roosevelt and wondered if Truman was ready for the presidency.

Truman's daughter, Margaret, described her father's feelings at that historic time:

> *Dad's first reaction was a tremendous surge of sympathy and grief. . . . His admiration for [Roosevelt] as a political leader, as the creator of the modern Democratic Party, was immense. No matter what office Dad held, he would have been grieved by the President's death. Now, in the presence of Mrs. Roosevelt's calm courage, and the awful knowledge of what the news meant to him personally, grief and awe and shock combined to create emotions of terrible intensity.*

To almost any American, following in the footsteps of a great leader like Franklin Delano Roosevelt would have seemed impossible. Yet this was the daunting task facing Harry Truman. At the moment, Truman was struggling to grasp the massive burden that had just been placed on him. The world was in the middle of the largest, most costly war in history. Millions of U.S. troops were fighting Nazi Germany in Europe. Millions more were stationed in the Pacific, battling imperial Japan.

Truman was unknown to most of the American public. He had been in office for only eighty-three days, serving as the new vice president as Roosevelt started his fourth term. Previously, Truman had served in the Senate for ten years. As a senator, he had been well respected by his colleagues for his honesty, fairness, and no-nonsense approach. But he was not a man who sought publicity. Writing in the *New York Times,* Alden Whitman described Truman as an ordinary

looking businessman, more at home in a small town than in
a big city. He looked "neat and plain," Whitman wrote. He
had "deep blue eyes that peered through steel-trimmed
glasses" and "an engaging smile."

On that misty, somber Thursday in 1945, Truman
found nothing to smile about. "But now the lightning had
struck," he wrote later, describing the moment of his ascent
in power. Flanked by his wife, Bess, daughter, Margaret,
cabinet members, and congressional leaders, Truman took
the oath of office from Chief Justice Harlan Stone in the
White House Cabinet Room. He looked "pleasant and sub-
stantial," Whitman noted. Still, reporters couldn't help
wondering—and writing—"Is he up to the job?"

*Truman took the presidential oath of office at 7:09 P.M., Thursday, April 12,
1945, becoming the thirty-third president of the United States. At sixty, he
inherited a world war and growing tensions with the Soviet Union.*

Truman's mother, Mattie, at about the time of Truman's presidency in 1945. A firm believer in Truman's abilities, she claimed that "it was on the farm that Harry got his common sense. He didn't get it in town."
✧ —————————

In the coming days, comparisons between Roosevelt and Truman filled the newspapers. Roosevelt's background of great wealth and prominence on the East Coast contrasted sharply with Truman's midwestern roots. Truman had been a farmer for many years of his life. He had never attended college. His family belonged to the Baptist church. Yet the lessons Truman learned while growing up on a Missouri farm (the value of hard work, honesty, and cooperation) had molded him into a man of strong character and judgment.

Those who knew Truman believed in him. When his mother heard that her son had become the thirty-third president of the United States, she was not at all surprised. Speaking of her son's strong work ethic, thoroughness, and attention to detail, she said, "I knew that boy would amount to something from the time he was nine years old. He could plow the straightest row of corn in the county. He could sow wheat so there wasn't a bare spot in the whole field."

CHAPTER TWO

FIELDS OF DREAMS

A farmhand, if he has an ample living, can be just as happy as a millionaire with homes in Maine and Florida.
—Harry S. Truman

The Truman trademark characteristics of hard work and honesty stemmed from Harry's grandparents, Mary Jane and Anderson Shippe Truman; and Harriet Louisa and Solomon Young. They were part of the great pioneer movement in America. They migrated from Kentucky to Missouri before the Civil War (1861–1865) and achieved their dream of owning and farming the fertile land there. Solomon Young's farm, called Grandview, was located about twenty miles south of Kansas City, Missouri. He named the farm after the railroad station nearby—one of the first in the state.

Grandview became a center for social activity—a favorite place for parties and dances. Neighbors enjoyed the chance to have fun after long hours of work on the farm.

Solomon and Harriet Louisa Young built the original Grandview farmhouse in 1844. That home burned to the ground fifty years later. Harriet Louisa and her son Harrison built a new, smaller home (above) in 1894.

On one such occasion, the Young's daughter Mattie met John Truman, son of Anderson and Mary Jane Truman. John and Mattie shared a love of music. John was a hard-working farmer who showed great respect for his fellow workers. But he had little patience with those who loafed on the job.

Except for some early country-school classes, John was uneducated. Mattie, however, had attended Lexington Baptist Female College, where she had studied piano.

She developed a love of reading there, too, which she shared with John.

FALLING IN LOVE

John and Mattie fell in love, and they married in 1881. They bought a small farmhouse in Lamar, a town in southwestern Missouri. The house had no running water and no indoor plumbing. But the new house was bright and sunny. John also bought a barn across the street, where he housed his mules. Hoping to become a successful livestock trader

Self-conscious of his height, John Truman sat for his wedding photograph (above) *to hide the fact that he was shorter than his wife, Mattie.*

like his father-in-law, he launched his mule-trading business
with an advertisement in a local newspaper:

Mules bought and sold. A lot of good mules.
Anyone wanting teams will do well to call on
J. A. Truman.

John and Mattie looked forward to starting a family,
too. But their first baby was stillborn. Then on May 8,
1884, in a room barely big enough for a bed, a healthy second baby was born. They named him Harry, after the
baby's uncle, Harrison, Mattie's brother. To honor both
grandfathers, Anderson Shippe Truman and Solomon
Young, Mattie and John gave Harry a middle initial—
S—instead of a middle name. The baby's full name was
Harry S. Truman. To mark the big occasion, John planted a
young pine tree in the front yard.

The Trumans welcomed Harry (left) to the world on May 8, 1884. Harry
(standing right) was joined by his brother John Vivian two years later.

The mule-trading business did not succeed. Soon after Harry's birth, John moved the family to a farm in Harrisonville, just a few miles from Solomon Young's farm. But the Truman farm failed to produce the profits John had hoped for, and once again, Mattie and John faced disappointment. Two years after the move, in 1886, Harry's younger brother John Vivian was born. Perhaps to distinguish between father and son, John Truman called the baby Vivian, as did others.

ON THE MOVE

With a larger family to support, the Trumans decided to move back to Grandview, the Young family farm in Jackson County. By that time, Solomon Young had become one of Missouri's most successful farmers. Solomon asked John to be his partner. The Youngs welcomed other family members to their large home, too. The family included John's father, Anderson Truman, whose wife had died a few years before. Harrison and Ada (Mattie's brother and sister), several cousins, hired hands, and visiting relatives also moved in. About fifteen people representing three generations lived together in the Young home.

Solomon Young

Acres of bluegrass, elm trees, strawberry patches, and a creek surrounded the sprawling Grandview house. Porches wrapped around the house and provided ample room for young Harry to play. Though he had toys to entertain him, he preferred chasing frogs, which made him laugh, and running through the prairie grass with his dog. Later he loved riding his Shetland pony around the farm, alongside Grandpa Young. Unlike his paternal grandfather Anderson Truman, who was quiet and reserved, Grandpa Young was outgoing and jovial. His long white beard reminded Harry of Santa Claus—a Santa Claus who rode on horseback! "Those were wonderful days and great adventures," Truman recalled years later.

CHAPTER THREE

FINDING HIS WAY

*While still a boy I could see that history had
some extremely valuable lessons to teach.*
—Harry S. Truman

The early years on the Young family farm were not all sun-
shine and pony rides. There were sad and traumatic times,
too. In 1887 Anderson Truman died. Harry was only three
years old at the time. Other events also affected his young
life. Once he fell off a chair and broke his collarbone.
Another time he nearly choked to death on a peach pit.
Mamma rescued him on both occasions. Harry adored his
mother. He seemed to recover from any mishap when she
read to him. Her reading was like a gift, he always said, and
before he was five, he was reading, too.

In 1889 Mamma gave Harry the best gift of all—
a baby sister. "From the sound of crying upstairs he and
Vivian thought a new pet had arrived," historian David
McCullough wrote. The girl's name was Mary Jane.

At the age of six, Harry's eyesight became a major problem. During a Fourth of July event near Grandview, the sounds of fireworks startled and excited him, but he showed no response to the colorful sparks that flashed across the sky. He couldn't see them.

Mattie made immediate plans to have Harry's eyes tested. Harry's father was away on a business trip at the time. Instead of waiting for her husband to return, Mattie hooked up two horses to the farm wagon and drove Harry fifteen miles to Kansas City to see an eye doctor. The doctor prescribed glasses for Harry—thick, wire-rimmed glasses. They changed his life forever. "I saw things and saw print I'd never seen before," he said. What had been fuzzy before was now perfectly clear to Harry. The doctor warned that he must not play any sports or do "any kind of roughhousing" for fear of breaking his expensive new glasses.

EARLY LESSONS

A boy who wore glasses in the farmyards of Missouri was unheard of in those days. Harry became something of a freak to others in the area. But Mattie and John were careful not to baby Harry or pity him because he looked different. He was punished for swimming in a mud hole with his brother Vivian. Once while riding with his father far out in the fields, Harry fell off his pony. John Truman made him walk all the way home. It was his father's way of reminding his son that anyone who couldn't stay on a horse did not deserve to ride one. Harry cried all the way to the house.

By the age of six, Harry was ready for school. The family moved to Independence, Missouri, a few miles from

*Possibly embarrassed about wearing his new glasses,
Truman (bottom left) did not wear them for many childhood
photographs, such as this one of his class at Noland School.*

Kansas City, because it was known for its good schools and public library. Since his mother had already taught him to read, Harry had a head start when he entered the Noland School in Independence. He liked his teachers and tried to please them. He later recalled, "I used to watch my mother and father closely to learn what I could do to please them, just as I did with my school teachers and playmates."

Harry hoped he would be judged by his behavior, not by how he looked. He refused to let his looks—his thick glasses in particular—become a barrier to friendship. Because of his small build and his eyeglasses, he avoided most sports, but he was an excellent student. A serious bout of diphtheria (a disease theat inhibits breathing) caused

Harry to miss half of the second grade. But with good tutoring by his mother, along with some summer school sessions, he not only made up for his missed time, but he also was allowed to skip third grade. Young Harry went straight to fourth grade in the fall.

Always at the top of his class, Harry sailed through school. He loved to read—especially books about great statesmen and military leaders, including Andrew Jackson and Robert E. Lee. "Say just what you mean," Lee wrote.

"Never do anything wrong to make a friend or keep one. . . . Deal kindly, but firmly with all your classmates. . . . Above all do not appear to others what you are not."

✧ ————————————
Truman learned admirable traits—including honor, honesty, and loyalty—from his family and childhood heroes, such as Robert E. Lee.

Honesty and frankness were Truman family traits. John Truman was known for both, and his son would be, too. But John was known for his hot temper as well. When kidded about his small size (he was five feet four inches tall), John was quick to react. He didn't hesitate to confront anyone who insulted him—with fists, if necessary! John Truman had great respect for women, and one would not dare speak rudely about any woman in his presence.

Like his father, Harry had deep respect for women, but in school, he was too shy to speak to most girls his own age. His best girl friends were two cousins, Ethel and Nellie Noland, who lived nearby. Ethel, who was four years older than Harry, was like an older sister to him. After school the three enjoyed acting out Shakespearean plays. "Harry was always fun," Ethel said.

At home Harry was surrounded by women—his mother, his younger sister, Mary Jane, Grandma Young, and various aunts who came to visit. Yet he remained shy around girls outside of his family. On one occasion, when he attended a Presbyterian Sunday school, instead of his usual Baptist church, Harry saw a particular young girl named Elizabeth (Bessie) Wallace, but was too shy to speak to her.

John and Mattie Truman encouraged Harry's love of books and music. They were as important to him as sports were to his friends. Piano lessons were customary for girls (but not boys) in Independence, but Harry didn't care if the boys in town thought playing music was girlish. He was thrilled to take lessons. He showed special talent, and his parents were proud of his ability to play. In those days before radio and television, almost anyone

Truman chose to wear his glasses for this photograph, taken about the time he was at the Columbian School.

✧ ————————————

who could afford a piano bought one. In growing communities like Independence, the piano was a symbol of prosperity.

Music was a part of the curriculum at the new Columbian School, which was built just a few blocks from the Truman house. Though Harry entered the new school with Ethel and Nellie, he felt lonely while adjusting to the different classrooms and teachers. He grew closer than ever to his cousins, who became a source of comfort.

When Harry was nine, Grandpa Young died. For the rest of his life, Harry often spoke of the "big man" with the flowing white beard who took him horseback riding around the farm. Both Grandpa Young and Grandpa Truman had been important figures in Harry's life. They formed the roots of his family tree and the core of his character.

CHAPTER FOUR

WHEN HARRY MET BESSIE

It's like old Mark Twain said, "Always do right. This will gratify some people and astonish the rest."

—Harry S. Truman

At the Columbian School, Harry sat directly in front of Bessie Wallace, the girl he'd seen at Sunday school, and he finally summoned the courage to speak to her. He even carried her books as they walked home from school together. For girl-shy Harry, this was a giant step forward. Bessie was not only pretty, with blonde hair and blue eyes, but she was a star athlete, too. Wherever she appeared—on the tennis court, baseball diamond, or skating rink—she was a major attraction.

Bessie was a Presbyterian, however, and Harry was a Baptist. In Independence there was a big distinction between the two religious denominations. As more people moved to Missouri from Kentucky, Tennessee, and the Carolinas, they brought their own prejudices with them—religious as well as racial. Presbyterians ranked at the top of the social order; Catholics, at the bottom; and Baptists, somewhere in between. Prejudice against Jews was prevalent, though there were few Jewish people in Independence at the time. Rarely, if ever, did the different denominations mix socially.

Church affiliation was not the only barrier Harry faced. Bessie was the dream girl of every boy in the class. Fortunately for Harry, optimism and perseverance were Truman trademarks.

Bessie Wallace

*Truman's first brush with politics
came during the 1892 presidential
election. He helped his father
organize a picnic to celebrate
Grover Cleveland's victory.*

THE WHOLE STORY IN A NUTSHELL!

Harrison's Ideas!

Cleveland's Ideas!

POLITICS
AND POETRY

Politics was a great unifier in Independence, a stronghold of the Democratic Party. The men and women of the community organized parades and other events to celebrate every Democratic victory. The most memorable one for Harry was the torchlight parade honoring Grover Cleveland's victory in the 1892 presidential election. Harry watched his father and others ride through town on horseback carrying torches held high, lighting up the town as they passed. During summer vacations, Harry and his brother Vivian helped their father harness the family mules and load up a wagon with food for the Democratic Party picnics in the nearby town of Lone Jack. Thousands of people came from all around the state to enjoy picnicking on the grass and listening to their favorite candidates promise even happier days to come.

But Independence was not a perfect American town. Nor was Missouri a perfect American state. In the post-Civil War years, America struggled with issues of race. Though Lincoln's Emancipation Proclamation had set slaves free from bondage, blacks were not free to go to the same schools, restaurants, or to sit in the front sections of trains with white people. In Independence, blacks were even banned from the public library.

Because the town was nearly an all-white community, segregation was not a big issue and was accepted as a natural way of life. But Harry had read about relationships between races in *The Adventures of Huckleberry Finn* by Mark Twain—one of his favorite authors. "What you want, above all things," Twain wrote, "is for everybody to be satisfied, and feel right and kind toward the others."

During his last few years in high school, Harry continued to study hard, and he earned praise from his teachers.

Throughout his life he credited his teachers for opening up new worlds for him—particularly through reading. From the poetry of Alfred Lord Tennyson to books by Mark Twain, Harry read everything he could get his hands on. But when he turned fourteen,

✧ ————————

Growing up, Truman learned valuable lessons from books. Mark Twain was one of his favorite authors.

he had a little less time to read because he added a paying job to his schedule.

Every morning, before school started, he cleaned the local drugstore before it opened. He arrived there at 6:30, and when he left for school, the place was as spotless as he could make it. Yet there were always some bottles left undusted, as he recalled years later:

> *There must have been a thousand bottles to dust and yards and yards of patent-medicine [non-prescription drug] cases and shelves to clean. . . . I never finished the bottles and shelves by schooltime and had to start the next morning where I'd left off the day before. By the time I got around them all, it was time to start over. How I hated Latin-covered prescription bottles and patent-medicine shelves!*

Harry was thrilled when he received his wages for his first week on the job. "I'll never forget my first week's wages—three big silver dollars. It was the biggest thing that had happened to me, and my father told me to save it for myself when I tried to give it to him."

Though Harry worked hard at both school and his job, nothing made him happier than playing the piano. He was overjoyed when his parents arranged for him to take lessons from Mrs. E. C. White in Kansas City. Her own teacher had been a teacher of Ignacy Paderewski, a world-famous pianist. Mrs. White introduced Harry to the works of such great composers as Bach, Beethoven, Chopin, and Mendelssohn—but it was the music of Wolfgang Amadeus

Truman (back row, fourth from left) *graduated from high school in 1901. He and Bessie* (second row, first from right) *are shown above in their senior photograph.*

Mozart that moved him most of all. Harry dreamed of becoming a concert pianist.

When Paderewski gave a concert in Kansas City, Harry couldn't wait to attend. After the performance, Mrs. White brought Harry backstage to meet the great artist. The master gave the young student some pointers about technique and style. It was a highlight of Harry's high school years.

In his senior year, Harry and some of his friends produced the school's first yearbook—*The Gleam*. The title came from the poem "Merlin and the Gleam" by the English poet Alfred Lord Tennyson. The poem was about searching for the "ideal light" to guide one through life. "Follow it," Tennyson wrote, "follow the gleam."

Harry graduated from high school on May 30, 1901, at the age of seventeen. He had survived the teasing from his classmates about his looks and his piano lessons. He had remained true to himself and earned the respect of his peers.

After graduation, his goal was to be admitted to the U.S. Military Academy at West Point, New York, or the U.S. Naval Academy at Annapolis, Maryland.

Harry wanted to learn more about the great military leaders he had read about and, perhaps, someday to become one himself. A career as a concert pianist still appealed to him, too. He was not sure which course he would take, but wherever he went, he hoped to win the heart of Bessie Wallace along the way.

CHAPTER FIVE

CALLED TO DUTY

I've always tried to get all the information I
could on every job I ever had. So nobody could
put anything over on me.
—Harry S. Truman

Because of his bad eyesight (without glasses), Harry's hopes
of entering either West Point or Annapolis were quickly
dashed. Other disappointments followed. His father had
invested the family's money in the Kansas City grain mar-
ket. The investments turned out badly, and John Truman
found himself with a huge amount of debt. Nineteen-year-
old Harry had to abandon his dream of college altogether.
Instead, he had to work full-time to help his father with
family expenses. He had to give up his piano lessons as
well, which erased any plans of becoming a concert pianist.
Yet Harry didn't complain. He knew it was his duty to help
his family.

After working in the mail room at the *Kansas City Star* newspaper, Harry took a better job as a timekeeper with the Santa Fe Railroad. He worked six days a week, ten hours a day, and earned thirty dollars a month. He called it a "down-to-earth" education. "Living with the labor gangs in their tent camps along the [Missouri] river," and listening to their foul language and "raw observations of life" showed Harry a part of America he never would have seen on a secluded college campus.

Following his railroad job, Harry and Vivian worked as clerks at the National Bank of Commerce in Kansas City. Harry worked in the vault, where he handled checks that sometimes totaled a million dollars a day. His salary in 1902 was forty-five dollars a month. Another young employee at the bank was Arthur Eisenhower, whose younger brother Dwight ("Ike") was in high school in Abilene, Kansas. Little did the bank manager know that he had a future president of the United States working for him—and a brother of another one!

─────────── ✧
Truman at about the time he clerked at the National Bank of Commerce in Kansas City

Truman served in Battery D of the Missouri National Guard Light Artillery.

✧ ————————————

While at the National Bank of Commerce, Harry lived at a boarding house nearby. He felt more and more like a businessman. When denied a raise at the bank, Harry went to work as an assistant teller at the Union National Bank, where he earned one hundred dollars a month. He also joined the National Guard in 1905. He was twenty-one years old. He passed the eye exam only because "they needed recruits," he said.

STAYING IN TOUCH

Harry kept in touch with his cousins Ethel and Nellie Noland. They occasionally came to Kansas City, bringing news of Independence with them. They attended plays and concerts with Harry in Kansas City. Harry loved the vaudeville shows at the Orpheum, too, and would sometimes usher there on weekends in order to see the shows for free. Vaudeville's fast-moving skits and slapstick comedy always made him laugh. However, life in Kansas City was not all laughs for Harry. In 1903 David Wallace, Bessie's father and one of the most prominent men in Independence, committed suicide. Though the tragedy was reported in the *Examiner,* the city newspaper, no one— including Harry—discussed it publicly. In those days, such a tragedy was kept private, especially when a drinking problem was involved, as it had been in David Wallace's case.

Bessie Wallace, her mother, and her siblings moved to Colorado for a year. When they returned, Bessie moved in with her mother and her mother's parents at 219 North Delaware in Independence. She commuted to the Barstow School—a private school for upper-class young women in Kansas City. Meanwhile, Ethel and Nellie Noland continued to keep Harry up-to-date about Bessie and other news of life in Independence.

———————————— ✧ ————————————

The Noland sisters were two of Truman's biggest supporters.
The two women, for example, kept him connected to Independence
and Bessie Wallace while he was away in Kansas City.

Truman returned to Grandview in 1905. He pitched in to help preserve the farm, taking on many responsibilities such as plowing fields.

In 1905 financial losses forced Harry's father to move his family to Grandma Young's farm in Grandview. With help from both Harry and Vivian, John Truman ran the farm there. Harry did not want to leave his job at the bank, but, again, he knew that duty called him home. "The family came first," David McCullough noted. "If Harry harbored any regrets or resentment, he never let on."

Harry learned every part of the farm operation and did every job well—so well, in fact, that when Grandma Young died and John Truman inherited the farm, he made Harry his partner. Vivian had married and moved to another farm nearby. Harry's ability to get along with others was as important as his job skills. When arguments erupted over Grandma Young's will, it was to Harry that everyone turned for solutions. He became known as the peacemaker in the family.

ON THE PLUS SIDE

The move to Grandview had a silver lining. The farm was only sixteen miles from Bessie Wallace's grandparents' house. Traveling there wasn't easy, however. Few trains stopped at Grandview, and streetcars required many transfers. Still, Harry visited Bessie whenever possible. Other young men courted her, too, but competition didn't stop Harry's pursuit of her. Bessie's mother, Madge Wallace, was not pleased with Harry's pursuit. "That farmer boy... is not going to make it anywhere," she told Bessie.

Truman (front seat) *attempted to woo Bessie Wallace* (front seat) *by writing her many letters and taking her on dates such as this picnic drive.*

To Mrs. Wallace, whose parents' house on Delaware Street was perhaps the largest and most elegant in Independence, the Truman farm in Grandview was backwoods country. In addition, Madge Wallace depended on Bessie to comfort her in the awful aftermath of her husband's suicide and the lasting stigma attached to it. She would have objected to any young man who seriously courted her daughter at that time. She idolized Bessie and thought no man was good enough for her. But Ethel and Nellie Noland were greatly impressed by Harry. Like cheerleaders, they rooted for him at every opportunity.

By 1910 Harry Truman was in love with Bessie. He wrote to her frequently. He wrote about his joining the

Masons—a brotherhood dating back to ancient times. He wrote to her about his background in literature, music, and farming. And he wrote about his feelings for her. Finally, in November 1913, Bessie told Harry that he was the

✧ ————————

Bessie Wallace in 1910. Though Truman lavished attention on her during this time, even creating a grass tennis court for her at Grandview, she was reluctant to visit him there.

only one she would consider marrying. When she repeated her promise in a letter to him, Harry, stunned and excited, wrote her back:

> *I know your last letter word for word and then I read it some forty times a day. Oh please send me another like it....I'm going to put it in a safety vault to keep from wearing it out. You really didn't know I had so much softness and sentimentality in me, did you? . . . I can tell you on paper how much I love you . . . but to tell it to you I can't. I'm always afraid I'd do it so clumsily you'd laugh. . . . Since I can't rescue you from any monster or carry you from a burning building or save you from a sinking ship—simply because I'd be afraid of the monsters, couldn't carry you, and can't swim—I'll have to go to work and make money enough to pay my debts and then get you to take me for what I am: just a common everyday man . . . who's anxious to be right.*

Harry would continue his correspondence with Bessie, often called Bess as an adult, while he helped his father run the farm at Grandview. In 1914, while trying to move a huge boulder from the road, his father suffered severe internal injuries and stomach damage. His condition worsened, and on November 2, 1914, John Truman died. His death marked a major turning point in Harry's life. Harry was on his own, and in a letter to Bess he expressed both his sadness and apprehension:

*You know, I've been in the habit of running the
farm for some time, but Papa always made it go.
He could make the men step lively even after he
was sick a great deal better than I can or ever
will. It surely makes me feel a loss that is quite
irreparable.*

Harry found that the healthiest way to cope with his
sadness was to keep busy. He joined his Uncle Harrison on
a trip to Texas in hopes of expanding his farm holdings.
His goal was to make enough money to marry Bess. But
financial losses began to plague him, delaying his marriage
plans. "My finances have seemed to put me farther from
that happy event [marriage]," he wrote Bess.

*Sometimes . . . I want to urge you to throw
prudence to the winds and take me anyway just as
things are and take a chance on my ever making
good and then I think of all the debts I'm saddled
with and of my present inability to even buy you a
decent ring and I haven't the nerve to do it.*

CHAPTER SIX

CAPTAIN HARRY

I never sit on a fence.
I am either on one side or another.
—Harry S. Truman

Hoping to get rich quick, Harry gambled his savings on a zinc and lead mine. The mine failed. Then, true to his optimistic nature, he invested in an oil company. He became secretary-treasurer of Morgan & Company Oil Investments. That company also failed. He then turned his attention to the National Guard.

Harry had stayed active in the Missouri National Guard, and when the United States entered World War I (1914–1918), he helped to expand part of the guard into a regiment. Though he was technically blind without his glasses, he memorized the eye chart, passed the test, and was accepted for active duty. He was elated about going overseas to serve his country, but Bess was worried that he

Hoping to strike it rich, Truman (above) partnered with Jerry Culbertson and David Morgan to form Morgan & Company Oil Investments.

might never come back. In fact, she was so worried that she asked him to marry her before he left. Marrying Bess had been Harry's longtime goal, but he didn't want to marry her and then leave her, so they agreed to wait.

THE MAKING OF A CAPTAIN
On March 30, 1918, Harry sailed to France. While training there, he rose to the rank of artillery captain. His unit was the 129th Field Artillery, a part of the Thirty-fifth Infantry Division. Harry led his battery of soldiers to victory in battles against German forces. "My battery fired three thousand rounds of ammunition from 4 A.M. to 8 A.M. on the morning the drive began," he wrote. "I had slept in the edge of a wood to the right of my battery position the night before, and if I had not awakened and got up early

that morning, I would not be here, for the Germans fired a barrage right on the spot where I had been sleeping."

Harry's battery included some of Missouri's wildest and roughest young men. Harry had met such types before while working on the railroad, and he knew how to work with them—straightforwardly and honestly. He soon earned their praise, and they called him Captain Harry.

His experiences in the war completely changed Harry's view of himself. He had led men through some of the bloodiest battles in world history, and he had led them to victory. He had become a leader. He was extremely proud of those who served under him—and of all the others in the Thirty-fifth Infantry Division. "The heroes are all in the infantry," he wrote to Bess. "There's nothing—machine guns, artillery, rifles, bayonets, mines, or anything else—that can stop them. . . . The Prussian Guards [enemy soldiers] simply can't make their legs stand when [they hear] the Yanks are coming."

———————————— ✧ ————————————

"Captain Harry's" World War I identity card

When the fighting finally ended on November 11, 1918, Harry couldn't wait to return to America to marry Bess. He was officially discharged from the army on May 6, 1919. He was thirty-five years old. Less than eight weeks later, on June 28, 1919, he and Bess were married in Independence. The couple lived with Bess's mother on Delaware Street so Bess could continue to take care of her.

Harry teamed up with an army buddy, Eddie Jacobson, to open a haberdashery—a men's clothing store—in nearby Kansas City. The two had worked together in a canteen during the war and looked forward to a partnership in business. After failing in his previous ventures— the zinc and lead mine and the oil company—Harry was determined to make Truman & Jacobson, as the establishment was called, a big success. "The idea of a haber- dashery was Eddie's,

✦ ————————

Harry and Bess Truman were married at 4 P.M. on Saturday, June 28, 1919, in Independence, Missouri. The tiny, crowded church became so hot that the wedding flowers wilted.

and it was agreed that he would be the buyer and I would act as salesman," Harry wrote in his *Memoirs.*

Harry loved conversing with customers, and they responded to his direct, enthusiastic approach. The clientele was a mixture of old and new residents. Kansas City had become a large center of activity in Missouri. Jazz bands attracted people from around the state. They were especially drawn to Twelfth Street, which was made famous by "The Twelfth Street Rag," a popular song of the day. And Truman & Jacobson was located conveniently on that street—a street that became a symbol of the Jazz Age that characterized the 1920s.

The "swinging" atmosphere in Kansas City also created a draw for gamblers and prostitutes as well as fun-loving citizens—including some of Harry's old army pals. At the same time, old prejudices—especially anti-Semitism (hostility towards Jews)—were still alive in the area. They deepened as more people from various backgrounds moved to the state. For example, when Bess wanted to invite Eddie Jacobson for dinner, her mother would not allow her to do so because Eddie was Jewish. But his mother-in-law's refusal to let Eddie in the house did nothing to dampen Harry's friendship with his partner. He knew that Eddie was a good person, and without brave men like him, the United States and its allies—Great Britain, France, and others—could not have won World War I.

BUILDING BRIDGES TO THE FUTURE

Truman & Jacobson started out successfully. But as the country's economy struggled following the war, the business began to suffer. As their store rent increased and debts grew larger, the two friends finally had to close the store in 1922. It was one of countless business closures during that time, and Harry would spend decades paying off his debts.

But even before Truman & Jacobson shut down, Harry was already in search of a new career. Jim Pendergast, another army friend, suggested that Harry apply his skills to politics. Though Jim was a loyal friend, he was also part of the notorious Pendergast political "machine"—a powerful family that promoted gambling, prostitution, and bootlegging (illegal selling of alcohol) in Kansas City. The Pendergasts also had a knack for recognizing—and promoting—potential political candidates.

Founded by James Pendergast Sr., the machine's operations were carried on by his sons, Jim, Tom, and Mike. They were masters at influencing elections for their friends in the Democratic Party—even if they stuffed ballot boxes to do so.

The family had been impressed by John Truman's fine reputation as well as Harry's own popularity in the community. They thought Harry's popularity among veterans, in particular, could win him an election. As long as Harry had no connection to the hate-infested, racist, anti-Catholic Ku Klux Klan, Mike, Tom, and Jim Pendergast agreed that he would be an acceptable candidate for eastern judge of Jackson County. They offered to back him 100 percent. Harry took their advice and won his first elective office.

The title of eastern judge was not a judgeship in the usual sense. He did not preside over court cases, but rather he held jurisdiction (authority) over the county highway department.

Truman accomplished much-needed rebuilding and repair of Missouri's roads and bridges and saved taxpayers money in the process. Like his father, Harry had a talent for spotting—and eliminating—waste. He applied attention and money only where it would benefit the most people. "To be called 'Judge' pleased Harry immensely," David McCullough noted. "He enjoyed the prestige of the job and the way people greeted him as he walked briskly to and from the courthouse." It was like being Captain Harry again.

Though he was always loyal to his friend Jim Pendergast, Harry refused to take bribes or do anything illegal to win votes or to try to stay in office—practices that typified the Pendergast and many other political machines. Rising above such practices at that time in Kansas City was not easy for Harry, but he did it. His reputation for honesty and integrity became widespread.

But more important than any elective office was the birth of Harry and Bess's first and only child, Mary Margaret, whom they called Margaret. Margaret was born on February 17, 1924. The birth "was, with the exception of his wedding day, the biggest event of [Harry's] life thus far," McCullough wrote. She was the center of attention

A proud and happy Truman holds his infant daughter, Mary Margaret.

among all the relatives, too, including Ethel and Nellie Noland who lived down the street. "For Harry, on the verge of forty," McCullough wrote, "life had new meaning." And friends noted that "his face just beamed."

Margaret's arrival brought the joy Harry needed as he faced defeat in his reelection bid as judge in Jackson County. The powerful Ku Klux Klan was "unalterably opposed" to Truman and spoke out strongly against him. Truman lost the election to the Republican nominee, Henry Rummel. Once again he was out of a job—but not for long. With typical Truman zeal, he went to work for various organizations, including the Kansas City Automobile Club. He became president of the nonprofit National Old Trails Association, which promoted tourism in Missouri. At the same time, he kept in close touch with the Pendergasts. With their support, Harry ran for office again, this time for a position with more authority than his last public office—presiding judge.

Harry won the judgeship in 1926, and he served two four-year terms between 1927 and 1935. His honesty and no-nonsense approach to all matters was like a fresh breeze across Missouri. The *Independence Examiner* took note: "No criticism or scandals of any importance have been brought with the county court as a center and no political charges of graft and corruption have been made against it." The *Kansas City Star* praised Truman's "enthusiastic devotion to county affairs." A *St. Louis Star-Times* editor praised his ability to "discuss administrative problems on an equal basis with visiting experts."

Harry's leadership qualities became evident as he announced his intentions on his first day in office:

Truman (second from right) *takes the oath of office for presiding judge of Jackson County. Opponents tried to prevent the day from ever happening. Some, it is believed, went so far as attempting to kidnap young Margaret.*

◇

> *We intend to operate the county government for the benefit of the taxpayers. While we were elected as Democrats, we were also elected as public servants. We will appoint all Democrats to jobs appointable, but we are going to see that every man does a full day's work for his pay. In other words we are going to conduct the county's affairs as efficiently and economically as possible.*

As Harry became known for his high standards, the Pendergasts' reputation for corruption was spreading. Could Truman ever run for—and win—a higher office while tied to the Pendergast machine? As reporters debated that question, Truman remained optimistic.

CHAPTER SEVEN

ESCAPING THE SHADOW

There's an old joke that the vice president's principal chore is to get up in the morning and ask how the president is feeling.

—Harry S. Truman

Believing that Harry could gain the trust of Missourians all across the state, the Pendergast machine went into high gear, helping him win a seat in the U.S. Senate in 1934. Yet because of his connection to the corrupt politics in his home state, his arrival in the nation's capital was anything but friendly. In fact, some senators refused to speak to him. No matter how hard Truman worked or how popular he became, the Pendergast shadow followed him. To make matters worse, Bess hated the attention from the media in Washington, D.C., and made return visits to Independence as often as possible.

Margaret, then ten years old, was not happy about moving from a spacious house in Independence to a four-room apartment in Washington, but when Harry surprised her with a piano, she was overjoyed. Her early love of music thrilled her parents, especially her father.

Truman was determined to do his best on behalf of his constituents and the country. When he took office, the entire nation was in the middle of the Great Depression. This period of crippling economic despair saw thousands of businesses go bankrupt and millions of people lose their jobs, homes, and savings. Truman

The Truman family, 1934
───── ◇ ─────

aligned himself with President Franklin Delano Roosevelt's programs—the New Deal—that had been designed to pull America out of its economic difficulties. As he did in Missouri, Truman investigated areas of waste in both business and government. In doing so, he uncovered corruption and fraud in the railroad industry and overspending on defense (military and arms production) contracts, saving the government millions of dollars.

WORLD WAR II

By the 1940s, Truman had earned the respect of his colleagues and at last had begun to step out of the Pendergast shadow. His keen eye for misconduct and waste had earned

*The Japanese surprise attack on Pearl Harbor devastated the
U.S. Navy and drew the country into war.*

him the chairmanship of the congressional committee that
probed spending on defense projects. His special group was
called the Truman Committee. Its formation was well
timed, because, on December 7, 1941, the Japanese
attacked Pearl Harbor, the United States naval base on the
southern coast of Oahu, one of the Hawaiian islands. The
attack brought about America's entrance into World War II.
With the country at war, overseeing defense contracts
became more important than ever.

Truman's organizational skills, combined with his ability to recognize and develop the potential of each committee member, made him a popular chairman. "As nearly as I
could, I distributed the work so that every member of the
Committee found his special abilities challenged to the
utmost," he wrote later. It was Captain Harry bringing out
the best in those who served him.

The Truman Committee faced a variety of complaints
as well as challenges, as described in Truman's *Memoirs:*

There were manufacturers who felt that their products had been discriminated against. There were producers who complained that they could not get priorities for their products. There were industrialists who accused competitors of using their official positions . . . for private gain. And there were small businessmen who complained that they could not get government contracts for their services and products, which would be helpful in winning the war.

Truman's careful watch of defense spending saved the country approximately $15 billion and earned him high praise in Congress. Until 1944 President Roosevelt had known little about Truman except for his embarrassing ties to the notorious Pendergast machine. But now the president had good reason to praise him for his fine record in the Senate. Democratic Party officials urged Roosevelt to consider Truman as his vice president in the upcoming 1944 election. But Truman

─────────────✧

Senator Truman headed up the Truman Committee, keeping an eye on military spending and the quality of military supplies manufactured for the war effort.

did not want to be vice president. He was happy in the Senate, where he could work quietly, out of the limelight. Bess Truman worried about the additional media attention should her husband become vice president. Also, she was afraid that her father's suicide—a fiercely guarded family matter—would be fodder for reporters.

Running for an unprecedented fourth term, Roosevelt (and most Americans) believed that leadership should not change during wartime. Under Roosevelt's guidance, in concert with America's major allies (Great Britain, the Soviet Union, and others), the war was nearly won.

ANSWERING THE CALL TO DUTY—AGAIN

Democratic Party leaders debated the winning qualities of other potential vice presidential candidates, including Henry Wallace, vice president at the time, and James Byrnes, former associate justice of the U.S. Supreme Court. Roosevelt was finally swayed by those who favored Truman. It was Truman's fine reputation that most appealed to Roosevelt. To pin down Roosevelt's choice quickly, Bob Hannegan, Democratic Party chairman, asked the busy president for a written endorsement of Truman. On the back of an envelope the president wrote simply: "Bob, I think Truman is the right man. FDR."

Truman insisted he was not a candidate and supported James Byrnes for the post. Byrnes, Truman thought, would be Roosevelt's ultimate choice. At the time, Roosevelt was preoccupied with the war overseas and showed little interest in the vice presidency. His health was failing, too, though his condition was not apparent in public.

During the Democratic National Convention in July, Roosevelt repeated his choice of Truman to party officials, but Truman was still not convinced. He wanted a more direct confirmation from the president himself. Bob Hannegan then telephoned Roosevelt as Truman listened.

"Bob," Roosevelt said, "have you got that fellow [Truman] lined up yet?"

"No," Hannegan replied. "He's the contrariest Missouri mule I've ever dealt with."

Then, Truman heard the president say, "Well, you tell him, if he wants to break up the Democratic Party in the middle of a war, that's his responsibility."

Stunned, Truman finally was convinced. "Well," he told Hannegan, "if that is the situation, I'll have to say yes, but why . . . didn't he tell me in the first place?"

Truman had a private luncheon meeting with President Roosevelt in August 1944. During the meeting, Truman noticed troublesome signs of the president's physical condition. He later told close friends that "the President's hands shook so badly at the luncheon that he could not get the cream from the pitcher into the coffee." The president's failing health was kept a closely guarded secret.

Truman did most of the campaigning for the Roosevelt-Truman ticket in 1944, so the president could focus on winning the war and improving his health. To no one's surprise, Roosevelt and Truman easily defeated their Republican opponents, Governor Thomas E. Dewey of New York and Senator John W. Bricker of Ohio.

Truman looked forward to making the best of his role as vice president. "The man who fills the office can choose to do little or he can do much," the vice president wrote.

Leading up to Truman's vice presidential swearing-in ceremony (above) was his sweeping nomination at the Democratic National Convention in July of 1944. Truman greatly surpassed candidates Henry Wallace and William O. Douglas with 1,031 delegational votes to their combined 105.

———————————— ✧ ————————————

Though Roosevelt did not involve Truman in policy making or take him into his confidence, he was sure of Truman's qualifications. As Roosevelt had told Bob Hannegan, Truman was the right man for the vice presidency.

But the sudden death of President Roosevelt of a cerebral hemorrhage (ruptured blood vessel in the brain) on April 12, 1945, thrust Truman into the presidency itself. Barely into his job as vice president, Truman had now become president of the United States. "I felt the moon, the stars, and all the planets had fallen on me," he told reporters.

CHAPTER EIGHT

PRESIDENT TRUMAN

*I am getting ready to see Stalin and
Churchill; and it is a chore. I have to take
my tuxedo, tails . . . preacher coat, high hat,
low hat and hard hat.*

—Harry S. Truman

Perhaps no president in American history was mourned as
deeply as Franklin Delano Roosevelt. He had served as president for more than twelve years (1933–1945). No president had spent as many years in office. No president before
Roosevelt had faced such an array of challenges. He had
dealt with an economic depression that had devastated the
country in the 1930s. He had led the United States into a
bloody war that sent young Americans into battles in North
Africa, Europe, and the Pacific in the 1940s. His New Deal
programs had put Americans back to work again and had
helped keep the nation afloat during desperate times.

And at the time of his death, American troops were already in Germany. It would be up to Harry Truman to assume the tremendous responsibilities of his predecessor.

Though Truman was respected in Congress, he was unknown to most of the country. In pre-television days, his face was unfamiliar. *Time* magazine reported: "Harry Truman is a man of distinct limitations. . . . In his administration there are likely to be few innovations and little experimentation." But Truman had no time to worry about such predictions. "Lightning had struck, and events beyond anyone's control had taken command," he said. His first thoughts were of Mrs. Roosevelt and her family. Truman assured Mrs. Roosevelt that "anything necessary to be done for [her family's] help and convenience would be done."

At the same time, Truman summoned the organizational skills that the president had praised him for. He called a meeting of Roosevelt's cabinet members (group of advisers) and asked them to remain in their respective offices. Like it or not, Truman was in command, and he would work hard and waste no time—as his hardworking father had taught him long ago.

Back at the Truman family apartment, the Secret Service had quickly taken their positions to guard the new president. Margaret, twenty-one years old at the time, recalled all the action following the public announcement of Roosevelt's death:

> *Secret Service men arrived to inform us that there was a big crowd gathering outside the apartment building. We went out the back door to avoid them, but some of the smart curiosity seekers*

were waiting for us there, along with numerous photographers. Flash bulbs exploded all around us. . . . Mother calmly ignored them. She steered me into the back seat of the car and we headed for the White House.

In the Cabinet Room of the White House, Harry Truman took the oath of office from Chief Justice Harlan F. Stone, becoming the thirty-third president of the United States. The awesome task of replacing President Roosevelt had begun. "As I took the oath of office I was conscious of how vast in scope the presidency had become," Truman noted.

─────────────── ✧ ───────────────

A solemn Harry S. Truman takes the presidential oath of office just hours after learning of the death of President Roosevelt.

President Truman (center) with Winston Churchill (left) and Joseph Stalin (right) during the Potsdam Conference in 1945. The Allied leaders met to discuss the future of a devastated and unstable postwar Europe.

⋄

A few weeks later, on May 7, 1945, Germany's remaining armed forces surrendered. Under the skillful command of General Dwight D. Eisenhower, the Allies had brought the war in Europe to an end. In July Truman met with the chief Allied leaders—Winston Churchill of Great Britain and Joseph Stalin of the Soviet Union—in Potsdam, Germany, to plan the future of postwar Europe.

The war in Europe had ended, but the continent lay in ruins. Questions about its recovery remained. Both Churchill and Truman knew that the military might of the Soviet Union had been crucial in the defeat of Germany. Yet both leaders distrusted Stalin and were concerned that he intended to take over as much of Eastern Europe as possible.

While in Germany, Truman wrote to Bess almost every day. "It made me terribly homesick when I talked with you yesterday," he wrote on July 29, 1945. "It seemed as if you were just around the corner, if six thousand miles can be just around the corner. I spent the day after the call trying to think up reasons why I should bust up the conference and go home."

While the fighting in Europe had stopped, war was still raging in the Pacific. At the Potsdam Conference, Truman was privately informed that the atomic bomb, the world's deadliest weapon, had been successfully tested at Alamogordo, New Mexico, on July 16. Within a month, it would be ready for use. The world at large knew nothing about this momentous event. Only those directly involved with the project knew about it. In fact, Truman himself had known little about the development of the bomb. Even when he was vice president, he had not been informed of the project. It would be his decision to drop the bomb—or not—on Japanese territory. After his return to Washington, D.C., from Potsdam, Truman discussed the vital matter with his closest advisers and experts on nuclear power.

PROS AND CONS

In typical Truman fashion, he listened to all points of view before making his decision to drop the atom bomb. His Joint Chiefs (military leaders) projected that an invasion of the Japanese mainland could lead to the loss of 250,000 or more American lives. Japanese soldiers did not believe in surrender. They fought to the death. Already the suicidal Japanese defenders of Okinawa, a small island chain south of the Japanese mainland, had caused 45,000 American casualties. In the end, 110,000 Japanese soldiers and 150,000 civilians had been killed or wounded there. To prevent greater loss of American lives and to bring the war to a quick end, Truman decided to authorize dropping the bomb on Japanese territory.

Those who opposed dropping the bomb were afraid that its power might extend far beyond the intended target.

They believed the bomb should be dropped on an unpopulated area—where its power would still be shocking enough to make the Japanese surrender. But American military experts were convinced that nothing but a major explosion on a military-industrial site would bring about a surrender from the Japanese.

On August 6, 1945, a U.S. plane dropped an atomic bomb on Hiroshima, a city on the island of Honshu, Japan, on the Inland Sea. Writing in the *New York Times,* World War II veteran Lester Bernstein recalled that monumental day:

> *I was a G.I. [soldier] who had weathered the war in Europe and now awaited my place in the storming of Japan's home islands. On Truman's orders, the first atomic bomb ever wielded in war exploded over Hiroshima. For Americans in uniform and those who waited for them to come home, outrageous as this may appear from the moral heights of hindsight, it was a sunburst of deliverance. . . . Today I know much more about Truman's decision, and for reasons that are not entirely selfish, I still think it was for the best.*

When Japan's military leaders refused to accept America's terms of unconditional surrender, a second bomb was dropped. It exploded on Nagasaki, a city on the Japanese island of West Kyushu. The blast killed 40,000 civilians and wounded 40,000 more. Having already lost 150,000 lives at Hiroshima, the Japanese finally accepted unconditional surrender less than a week after the bombings.

After the distinctive mushroom cloud (inset) *cleared from Hiroshima, the aftermath of the atomic bomb Little Boy was evident to the world.*

More than fifty years later, people continue to debate the question: Should the Japanese have been warned of the bombs' targets so that civilians would not be killed? Or, once warned, would the Japanese have placed American prisoners of war (POWs) in the targeted areas? As it turned out, an American invasion of the Japanese mainland had been averted, possibly saving hundreds of thousands of American lives. It was ironic, one reporter noted, that "a good and loving man decided to use the cruelest weapon in history."

"I never brooded over the decision to drop the bomb," Truman said. "It was not a question of right or wrong. It was a question of necessity." And it ended World War II.

CHAPTER NINE

TROUBLE ON THE HOME FRONT

If we do not abolish war on this earth, then surely,
one day, war will abolish us from this earth.
—Harry S. Truman

President Truman received the news of Japan's surrender on Tuesday, August 14, 1945. He went before the news-reel cameras in the White House and announced the news to the world. General Douglas MacArthur, commander of Allied forces in the Pacific, personally received the surren-der on September 2, 1945, onboard the USS *Missouri,* the United States battleship named after Truman's home state. After six long years, the bloodiest war in world history was over.

Celebrations began, and Bess and Harry Truman went to their private living quarters in the White House. Truman called his mother to tell her the news. "Harry's a wonderful man," she told a friend. "He always calls me after some-thing that happens is over."

A relieved President Truman announces Japan's unconditional surrender to an eager press and to the world.

And Truman indeed had earned such pride, as David McCullough noted:

> *In just three months in office Harry Truman had been faced with a greater surge of history with larger, more difficult, more far-reaching decisions than any President before him. Neither Lincoln after taking office, nor Franklin Roosevelt in his tumultuous first hundred days, had had to contend with issues of such magnitude and coming all at once.*

But even with the war at an end, there was no rest for Harry Truman. His work had only just begun. In the coming months, twelve million U.S. servicemen and women would be arriving home. Most of them would need new jobs and medical care. In addition, workers at home were tired of years of sacrifice—reduced wages, rationing of many goods— throughout the war. These people wanted wage increases and threatened to go on strike if they didn't get them. Truman presented legislation that he hoped would deal with these issues. But the spirit of unity and camaraderie that had existed among politicians of all parties during the war was gone. Many of Truman's ideas were disputed by Congress, but he pursued his agenda with a passion. Dealing with Congress was "like riding a tiger," he said. "A man has to keep riding or be swallowed."

To add to the new president's challenges, Bess was unhappy under the stress of her public role. She continued to return with Margaret to Independence for long stays. Truman was lonely without them. Once he even risked flying home in a blizzard to be with his family for Christmas. He thought his arrival would be a happy surprise. But Bess was furious that he had taken such a risk and wasted no time telling him so.

On his return to the White House, he wondered how he could be called the "No. 1 man in the world" by *Life* and *Time* magazines and be viewed as "something that the cat dragged in" on arriving home for Christmas! He wrote to Bess: "No one ever needed help and assistance as I do now. If I can get the use of the best brains in the country and a little help from those I have on a pedestal at home, the job will be done." (The letter, like many of Truman's, was later found in a drawer. It had never been sent. Writing about his feelings had always helped him to cope with them.)

The United Nations

Harry Truman vigorously supported the United Nations (UN), the organization established to maintain world peace and to foster solutions to the world's social, economic, cultural, and humanitarian problems. By joining the UN, the United States showed its determination not to isolate itself from international affairs, as it had done after World War I.

The United Nations was founded on October 24, 1945, with fifty-one founding members, including the United States. Most of the nations of the world are members of the United Nations. By bringing nations together to discuss their conflicts in a neutral setting, the UN has helped to avoid war on multiple occasions.

But Truman did even more than urge the creation of the United Nations. He nominated Eleanor Roosevelt, Franklin Delano Roosevelt's widow, as a delegate to the historic first meeting of the United Nations General Assembly in January 1946. She was the only woman to be included in the American delegation.

Truman's biggest challenge at this time was the threat of a strike by the nation's railway workers. Truman knew that such a strike would paralyze the country. Trains were critical to the nation's industry. They not only carried citizens across the country, but they transported food, clothing, medicine, and other necessities of life.

Truman's response to the issue was bold and controversial. When the workers organized and threatened to strike, Truman made a speech before Congress, threatening to draft the strikers into the army. Such a move would force the workers to continue working. Before the speech ended, he was told that the strike had been settled. Trains carrying vital goods to Americans continued to roll.

——————————————— ✧ ———————————————

Railroad workers check their watches, poised to carry out a threatened strike with the potential to shut down the nation.

*President Truman expressed his responsibility in his personal life
and in the presidency with the motto, The Buck Stops Here.*

TAKING A NOSEDIVE

The strike and its potentially disastrous effects had been avoided. But Truman's strong stance against the railroad workers alienated the nation's labor unions, who felt Truman had restricted their rights to demand better pay and working conditions. The country's union workers saw Truman as a man who did not support the common worker. Truman's popularity nose-dived. Yet he stood by his action, taking full responsibility. As the plaque on his desk stated: "The buck stops here." In other words, he would not "pass the buck"—or shift the blame or responsibility for his actions onto anyone else but himself.

He dealt with the stress of dropping popularity by taking brisk walks every morning and blowing off steam in his diary, letters, and occasionally to the press. Reporters loved his plain talk and swarmed around him on his daily walks.

In a letter to Margaret, who had embarked on a singing career, Truman gave his typical, straightforward advice regarding the important role of the press:

> *I want you to win on merit and I am sure you can win on merit—but if you do not have the proper representation of that merit no one will know of it. Hard work and a pleasant disposition will win. Remember, photographers are working people who sell pictures. Help them sell them. Reporters are people who sell stories—help them sell stories.*

By averting the railway strike, President Truman had inadvertently taken his own advice and helped reporters sell a big story.

Truman's job became even more difficult when Republicans won control of Congress in the 1946 national elections, creating more roadblocks for his policies. Nevertheless, he forged ahead and took strong political action again—this time against the Soviet Union's growing power in Eastern Europe.

Following World War II, Soviet armies had occupied much of Eastern Europe, including the nations of Bulgaria, Romania, Poland, Hungary, Czechoslovakia, and a section of eastern Germany. Postwar Germany had been divided into four zones. The four victorious allies—the United States, France, Great Britain, and the Soviet Union—each held authority over a zone. The Soviets controlled the northeastern part of the country, which was named East Germany. Soviet occupation allowed Soviet leader Joseph

Stalin to set up governments in the countries that were under his control. These Soviet-controlled governments were not democratic and did not hold free elections. The Soviet-controlled governments were also Communist. This meant they followed a system of government in which the government owns nearly all property and controls most aspects of citizens' lives. Citizens of these countries who spoke out against the Communist government risked imprisonment and possible execution.

Though Truman had liked Stalin at first and was optimistic about dealing with him in the future, their relationship quickly soured. The more Truman witnessed Stalin's appetite for power, the greater the gulf between them grew.

In 1947 Stalin attempted to expand his influence to other nations in Europe. Truman decided to make strong but peaceful moves to stop him. Because Communism is an economic system that claims to favor the poor, working-class citizen, it tended to flourish where people were poor and unemployed. At this time, the southeastern European nations of Turkey and Greece were vulnerable to Communist takeover.

Truman and many Americans felt that promises made by a powerful dictator like Stalin would be irresistible to such needy people. Truman planned to build up Europe economically and militarily in order to ward off a Soviet takeover. To accomplish his mission, he asked the Republican-led Congress to authorize millions of dollars in aid to help the governments of Turkey and Greece. He warned Congress of Stalin's aim to conquer Europe—to take away freedoms the Allies had fought so hard to keep in World War II.

Truman won his fight. Congress authorized $400 million to fend off Communism in Greece and Turkey. Truman's role as a leader had solidified, and the new multimillion dollar commitment was called the Truman Doctrine.

Next, Truman urged Congress to assist in rebuilding war-torn Western Europe, where many countries might be vulnerable to Soviet power. The plan called for $13 billion in aid to these nations. The Marshall Plan, as it was called, was named after Truman's new secretary of state, George C. Marshall, who had served as army chief of staff during World War II and had been instrumental in developing the plan. The program's passage in April 1948 was a great triumph for Truman.

✧ ————————————

President Truman (left) shakes the hand of Secretary of State George C. Marshall. Marshall was setting out for Europe to implement his plan for rebuilding the war-torn continent.

CHAPTER TEN

PRESIDENT TRUMAN, THE SECOND TIME AROUND

I believe that we must assist free peoples to work out their own destinies in their own way.

—Harry S. Truman

Truman enjoyed several successes in 1948. In that year, he became the first leader to recognize (formally acknowledge a country's political existence) the state of Israel, the new Jewish homeland. For centuries, the world's Jewish population had not had a home country. Though a homeland for the Jewish people had been supported by Great Britain decades earlier, such a country had never been established. During World War II, the German Nazi government had murdered more than six million Jewish people. This reign of terror, known as the Holocaust, had also left countless more European Jews homeless. Creating a homeland for these people was crucial. In 1948 the United Nations voted to divide the country of Palestine, on the eastern coast of the Mediterranean Sea, into Arab and Jewish regions. This region was the same region Jews had called home during biblical times. On May 14, 1948, Israel declared its independence and became the Jewish homeland.

That same year, Truman faced another confrontation with Stalin and the Soviet Union. The Soviet dictator attempted to seize control of West Berlin. Berlin, the pre-World War II capital of Germany, lay in the Soviet-occupied zone of eastern Germany. But the western half of the city was not controlled by the Soviet government. In 1948 Stalin sought to establish control over the other half of the city. To accomplish his goal, Stalin ordered his forces to blockade all roads, train routes, and water routes to West Berlin. The blockade cut off crucial materials such as food, clothing, and medicines to the city. The Soviet dictator hoped to starve the West Berlin population into accepting Soviet control.

The situation was hazardous. If Truman had responded to the blockade by threatening Stalin, another war might have started—perhaps even a nuclear war. But instead of confrontation, the United States and its allies chose a different tactic. They flew over the blockade. Over a period of months, hundreds of allied planes flew tons of supplies to West Berlin, thwarting Stalin's attempt to starve the city. Eventually Stalin lifted the embargo. Truman's clever—and peaceful—solution, known as the Berlin Airlift, won praise from all over the world. David McCullough called the Berlin Airlift "one of the most brilliant American achievements of the postwar era and one of Truman's proudest decisions."

German children wave at an allied supply plane (above). *During the Berlin Airlift, the United States, Great Britain, and France delivered more than 2.3 million tons of essential goods and supplies to the citizens of West Berlin.*

During his years as president, Truman worked to gain more rights for black Americans. In 1948 the U.S. armed forces were segregated, with most African American personnel serving in units separate from whites. Only a very small number of African Americans were in positions of authority in the military. As commander in chief of the armed forces, Truman ordered an end to this segregation. A year earlier, Truman had become the first American president to speak before the National Association for the Advancement of Colored People (NAACP)—an organization founded to work for the civil rights of African Americans. Truman's appearance before the NAACP showed he was serious about supporting the rights of African Americans. Many of Truman's other efforts to enact civil rights legislation failed, due mainly to strong opposition in Congress.

Truman also worked to improve the lives of America's elderly citizens. He recommended that Congress pass legislation for Medicare, a government program that helps pay for medical care for citizens aged sixty-five and older. Truman had first proposed Medicare in principle in 1945 and kept pursuing it. However, the legislation failed to pass Congress during his presidency. *Time* magazine's earlier prediction that "there are likely to be few innovations and little experimentation" in Truman's administration had clearly been put to rest.

While he made remarkable achievements in only a few years, Truman was always aware that his presidency was an accidental one. He had not been elected by the people but rather had automatically stepped into the role when President Roosevelt died. In 1948 it was time for Truman to run for office in his own right. His Republican opponent was Roosevelt's former challenger, New York governor Thomas E. Dewey.

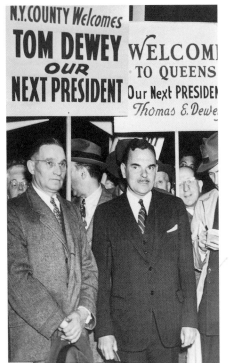

◇ ————————
Republican presidential candidate Thomas Dewey (right) poses for the cameras while campaigning.

Millions of Americans came out for President Truman's whistle-stop campaign (left). Despite the declarations of a hasty press (right), Truman won the election.

——————————— ✧ ———————————

To help him campaign, Bess and Margaret joined Truman on a whistle-stop train tour across the country. Truman traveled the country aboard the presidential train, the *Ferdinand Magellan,* stopping at various stations to deliver his campaign speeches directly to American voters.

Crowds gathered at Truman's campaign stops. "Give 'em Hell, Harry!" they shouted. The chant became a slogan for the campaign. Despite this, the election was extremely close. In fact, on the night of the election, the early edition of the *Chicago Daily Tribune* named Dewey the winner! DEWEY DEFEATS TRUMAN, the headline read.

But the newspaper was wrong. Truman had won. He had been elected president of the United States on his own—without the powerful aura of Roosevelt around him. Truman had won on his record of achievement, his honesty, straightforward talk, intelligence, and fair play. "But it would no more occur to him to gloat in victory than it would to gloom in defeat," Margaret said.

INNOVATIONS AND RENOVATIONS

On January 20, 1949, Truman was inaugurated on the East Portico of the White House. He was especially pleased to see in attendance some of "the boys" from Battery D who had served under his command in World War I. "They don't call me Mr. President," he told reporters. "They call me Captain Harry."

Truman accepted "with humility" the honor of being elected president by the American people. "I accept with a resolve to do all I can for the welfare of this nation and for the peace of the world." Later, he, Bess, and Margaret celebrated with thousands of others at the Inaugural Ball.

President Truman delivers his inaugural address on January 20, 1949.

ICELAND

NORTH
ATLANTIC OCEAN

FINLAND

NORWAY

SWEDEN

UNITED
KINGDOM

SOVIET UNION

DENMARK

NETHERLANDS

IRELAND

GERMAN
DEMOCRATIC
REPUBLIC

FEDERAL
REPUBLIC
OF
GERMANY

POLAND

BELGIUM

LUXEMBOURG

CZECHOSLOVAKIA

FRANCE

AUSTRIA

HUNGARY

SWITZERLAND

ITALY

ROMANIA

Black Sea

YUGOSLAVIA

BULGARIA

PORTUGAL

SPAIN

TURKEY

ALBANIA

GREECE

Mediterranean Sea

Non-NATO Countries

Joined NATO in 1952

Charter Members of NATO, 1949 (United States and Canada not shown)

Truman, who was not a dancer, waved to the crowds from the balcony of the ballroom and enjoyed watching them dance the night away. He loved every minute of it, Margaret noted, and his face was "shining like a new moon."

Once the parties ended, Truman settled into his elected post as president. As he had promised in his inaugural speech, he would do all he could for the peace of the world. A major step in that effort was the signing of the North Atlantic Treaty on April 4. The North Atlantic Treaty Organization (NATO) joined together the United States, Canada, and ten Western European nations in a defense pact. If any one country was attacked, all others would respond. NATO was created to discourage the Soviet

Union from any attempts at aggression. To Truman, NATO was as important as the Marshall Plan.

Truman also outlined his Point Four program—a plan to share scientific and industrial knowledge with the under-developed nations of the world. Truman believed that it was the duty of rich nations to help poor ones. Arnold Toynbee, a noted British historian, called Truman's bold plan "the signal achievement of the age."

In November 1950, the Truman family moved into Blair House, across the street from the White House, while much-needed renovation and repairs of the White House took place. Floors of the old building had been weakening, and parts of ceilings had collapsed. In fact, one of two pianos in a room above the family dining room had fallen through the floor! Truman noted in his diary-calendar, "How very lucky we are that the thing did not break when Margie and [family friend] Annette Wright were playing two-piano duets."

But White House construction problems were only part of the turmoil Truman faced at the time. Military action in Korea, a country in northeastern Asia, cast a dark shadow over the summer of 1950. Truman's strong leadership quali-ties would be put to the test. The conflict on the Korean Peninsula once again pitted the United States and its allies against Stalin and the Soviet Union, though indirectly. An escalation of the fighting could ignite World War III. It would be up to Truman, in concert with the United Nations, to make sure such a disaster did not happen.

CHAPTER ELEVEN

TAKING CHARGE, TRUMAN STYLE

*The president gets a lot of hot potatoes from every
direction . . . and a man who can't handle them has
no business in that job.*

—Harry S. Truman

The Korean Peninsula was under Japanese control from 1895
to the end of World War II in 1945. Following the war,
Soviet troops occupied the northern half of the country,
while the U.S. military occupied the south. The United
States and the Soviet Union tried to negotiate to reunite the
country, but these negotiations failed. Eventually, U.S. and
Soviet forces left Korea. A Communist government was set
up in what became North Korea, while a democratic government was formed in the southern half of the country.

On June 25, 1950, Communist North Korea invaded
South Korea. Truman found himself and the world in
another difficult situation. The Communist North Koreans

were backed by the Soviet Union. The United Nations protested North Korea's actions. When the North Koreans refused to withdraw from South Korea, the UN sanctioned war against North Korea. Since both the Soviet Union and the United States had developed atomic bombs by then, Truman's decision to send troops to Korea was a crucial one. Any military conflict between the two powers had the potential of starting a nuclear war. Truman chose General Douglas MacArthur, victorious leader in the Pacific during World War II, to head the armed forces in South Korea. MacArthur was a popular figure, greatly admired for his accomplishments in the Pacific. When the general assured Truman that the war in Korea would be over by Christmas, Truman was relieved.

During the escalating conflict in Korea, two Puerto Rican men attempted to assassinate Truman at Blair House on

Marines spearhead the attack, as the first U.S. forces go into action near Pusan, South Korea, on August 2–3, 1950.

Assassin Oscar Collazo lies wounded but alive after attempting to shoot his way into Blair House.
——————— ✧

November 1, 1950. By killing the president, the men hoped to bring attention to the Puerto Rican independence movement. The assassination attempt was quickly thwarted by Blair House guards, although one guard was killed. One of the Puerto Ricans was killed, and the other was sentenced to die in the electric chair. As a goodwill gesture to the people of Puerto Rico, Truman commuted the sentence to life imprisonment.

The death of the Blair House guard deeply affected Truman. He started a fund to provide financial assistance to the family of the man who had been killed protecting him. "You can't understand just how a man feels when somebody else dies for him," he said.

Truman's regard for the feelings and needs of others drew praise from those who worked for him. His respect for others came through in his day-to-day office procedures. Truman hated to summon an aide from his desk in the Oval Office. Instead, he preferred to greet him or her personally at the door of the office. "This constant consideration for others, the total lack of egotism . . . was the real source of the enormous loyalty he generated in those around him," Margaret Truman wrote.

A Man of Honor and Fair Play

Examples of President Truman's thoughtfulness and sense of fairness abound. But one example during the Korean War stands out.

Truman read in a newspaper one morning that the body of Sergeant John Rice, an American soldier killed in action in Korea, had been sent to Sioux City, Iowa, for burial. But before the casket was actually lowered into the grave, the Sioux City Memorial Park officials ordered the ceremony to stop. They announced that Rice was a Winnebago Indian and not "a member of the Caucasian race." Therefore, his burial would not be allowed.

Truman was outraged. He quickly arranged for Sergeant Rice to be buried in Arlington National Cemetery with full military honors. And he sent an air force plane to bring Rice's widow and her three children to Washington for the ceremony.

Fortunately, there were family events to help Truman take his mind off pressing problems both at home and abroad. He especially looked forward to a concert Margaret was giving at Constitution Hall in Washington, D.C. Critics had praised Margaret's debut as a singer, saying she showed real promise. And she was the first daughter of a president to choose a professional career rather than the comforts of White House living.

On the night of the concert, December 5, 1950, Charlie Ross, Truman's boyhood friend and loyal secretary, died suddenly of a heart attack. Saddened and shocked, he still attended his daughter's concert. David McCullough described the memorable night:

> When Margaret came on stage, radiant in pink satin, and made her bow to the presidential box, Truman smiled and applauded. No president had ever been such a frequent concertgoer in Washington. He was a "regular" at Constitution Hall, at times, if the program included Mozart or Chopin, bringing the score with him. But tonight, even with his "baby" on stage, Truman looked extremely downcast.

The *Washington Time-Herald* said that she sang better than ever before and that her voice was "charming." But that was not the review that Truman saw first thing the next morning. Instead, he read the review in the *Washington Post* by critic Paul Hume. Hume called Margaret's voice "of little size and fair quality." Though he called her "extremely attractive on stage," he said "she could not sing very well [and] was flat a good deal of the time." Then he added: "There are few moments during her recital when one can relax and feel confident that she will make her goal, which was to end the song." The insult, coupled with the grief of losing his close friend, was too much for Truman.

As Margaret had once noted, her father "could match his sparks against the greatest temper losers in White House history . . . if the circumstances warranted." And Truman proved it by writing a scathing note to Hume, which made national headlines:

When you write such poppy-cock as was in the back section of the paper you work for it shows conclusively that you're off the beam and at least four of your ulcers are at work. Some day I hope to meet you. When that happens you'll need a new nose, a lot of beefsteak for black eyes, and perhaps a supporter below!

Many believed that Truman was letting off steam in the wake of Charlie Ross's death. Had Ross been alive, it is believed that the message never would have reached Hume's desk. Ross wouldn't have allowed it to be sent. In fact, Truman agreed (privately) that he never should have written the letter, but once printed in public, he stood by it.

BOLD DECISIONS

Back at work, Truman had to deal with a different kind of public disagreement—this time, from General Douglas MacArthur. During the latter months of 1950, UN forces under MacArthur's command drove the North Korean forces back into the northern part of the peninsula. Meanwhile, Truman had given his commander explicit orders to keep the war confined within Korea's boundaries. But in late November 1950, troops from neighboring Communist China joined the battle against UN forces. In response, MacArthur wanted to invade the mainland of China, thus widening the war. Truman vehemently disagreed. He wanted no part of such an invasion—one that could ignite a world-wide war in the age of nuclear weapons.

Ignoring Truman's role as commander in chief, MacArthur grew more critical of Truman's orders and even spoke out

General MacArthur receives a hero's welcome after being relieved of command in 1951.
——————————— ✧

against the president in public. Truman had no choice but to fire General MacArthur for insubordination (disobeying his commander in chief). In his characteristic manner, Truman had consulted with numerous high-level officials before coming to a decision. All of his high-ranking military leaders agreed that MacArthur should be fired. An admiring American public, however, was outraged.

MacArthur received a hero's welcome on his return home. He gave a memorable speech before Congress in which he explained his views and his actions in Korea. He ended the speech with the now-famous line, "Old soldiers never die, they just fade away." Though privately Truman called the speech nonsense, he publicly thanked MacArthur for his long term of outstanding service to his country.

Truman's response to the situation demonstrated his straightforward approach. When Cabell Phillips of the *New York Times* asked Truman if it took courage to fire MacArthur, Truman replied, "Courage had nothing to do with it. He was insubordinate and I fired him, and that's all there was to it. Sure, I knew there would be a lot of stink about it. But it was the right thing to do and I did it."

Although peace talks began in 1951, battles continued in Korea for two more years, with territory changing hands. Under General Matthew Ridgway's command, the Communist forces were finally pushed out of South Korea. The war ended where it had began—on Korean soil—with North Korea and South Korea divided at the thirty-eighth parallel as agreed to by the Allies after World War II. A possible third world war had been averted.

Truman went on to tackle the threat of a strike by the nation's powerful steel industry. Like the earlier railroad strike threat, a strike by steelworkers would cripple the country. Such a halt in production—especially while armed forces were still in Korea and in need of equipment— seemed outrageous to Truman. Once again, he took bold action and seized the steel mills, which meant that the mills would be under government control. His strong move inflamed the business community. Truman explained his action and defended its legality to the American people:

> *If we knuckle under to the steel industry, the lid would be off, prices would start jumping all around us—not just the prices of things using steel but prices of many other things we buy, including milk and groceries and meat.*

But the steel industry challenged Truman in court. The U.S. Supreme Court decided that Truman had overstepped his power. Steelworkers went on strike—a strike that lasted seven weeks. Truman was forced to approve a rise in steel prices. Yet he maintained that his actions had been per- fectly justified.

CHAPTER TWELVE

"SO LONG, HARRY!"

I wasn't one of the great presidents, but I had a good time trying to be one, I can tell you that.
—Harry S. Truman

To Bess Truman, the decision that her husband made on March 29, 1952, was perhaps the best one of all. On that day, Truman told the nation he would not run for reelection. He explained his decision not to run for president again:

> *I have tried my best to give the nation everything I have in me. There are a great many people. . . who could have done the job better than I did. But I had the job and I had to do it. . . . I always remember an epitaph [in] the cemetery at Tombstone, Arizona. It says: "Here lies Jack Williams. He done his damndest." I think that is the greatest epitaph a man can have.*

Truman's decision not to seek reelection elated his wife. "Bess looked like Harry did when he drew four aces!" one of his poker playing friends said.

HOUSEWARMING

That same month, the Trumans moved back to the newly renovated White House, which opened to the public in April. On May 3, Truman led a televised tour of the beautifully remodeled building. "His poise, his naturally hearty laugh, and his intuitive dignity made for an unusual and absorbing video experience," Jack Gould of the *New York Times* wrote. Truman surprised the audience by spontaneously sitting down at the piano and playing some Mozart. He had no script. He didn't seem to need one.

—————————————— ⬧ ——————————————

President Truman (right) shows reporter Walter Cronkite (left) the Diplomatic Reception Room during the first public television tour of the White House in 1952.

*The Truman family portrait was painted during
President Truman's last months in office.*

─────────── ✧ ───────────

He was "at his best," David McCullough noted, at once "amusing" and "knowledgeable."

The Trumans were extremely popular with the White House staff. Bess Truman was as concerned about the welfare of others as her husband was. Before air-conditioning was installed in the building, Bess would often tell the servants to stop working on hot days. Even "if it wasn't hot," one servant recalled, "she'd say, 'You've been working too long. Stop now....' [She] would order, yes *order* [us] to rest."

President Truman was especially interested in the welfare of children. Before he left the White House, he decided to spend the rest of his life "in large measure teaching young people the meaning of democracy as exemplified in the Republic of the United States."

Truman's last months in office, prior to the 1952 presidential election, were filled with farewell dinners, including one at the British Embassy, given by his old friend and wartime ally, Winston Churchill. Truman was praised by members of Congress for his innovative programs and actions that had made the country and the world a more humane place. These included the Truman Doctrine, the Marshall Plan, the Berlin Airlift, NATO, recognition of the new state of Israel, and his strong support of the United Nations.

He received praise from newspapers around the country. Cabell Phillips of the *New York Times* wrote: "He was the sort who synthesized the awesome responsibilities of his office not in resonant phrases that would look good in bronze, but with a simple, homespun aphorism: Tapping his desk and looking solemn as a preacher he would say, 'The buck stops here.'"

Though most Americans seemed to appreciate Truman's homespun ways, some did not. They thought his language was often too brash or crude and that he failed to bring style and grace to the White House.

However, one group in particular appreciated President Truman exactly as he was—the reporters who covered him. "No president of the last 50 years was so widely and warmly liked by reporters as Mr. Truman," Cabell Phillips noted. They relished their access to him—especially the after-hours poker games he often played with them.

Truman endorsed Adlai Stevenson, governor of Illinois, as the 1952 Democratic presidential candidate. Stevenson had the style and grace many Americans seemed to be looking for. But it was a Republican, the popular war hero Dwight D. Eisenhower, who won the election that fall to become the thirty-fourth president of the United States.

Republicans and Democrats alike applauded Truman's farewell speech. In it he predicted a change in world politics

President Truman (left) *congratulates president-elect Dwight D. Eisenhower and vice president-elect Richard Nixon* (far right) *on their victory.*

and the end of the hostilities between America and the Soviet Union. "Whether the Communist rulers shift their policies of their own free will—or whether the change comes about in some other way—I have not a doubt in the world that a change will occur." At the time, few could imagine an end to the hostility between the Soviet Union and the United States, but the eternally optimistic Harry Truman could.

After a farewell luncheon—a private event that included cabinet members, aides, and close friends—the Trumans boarded the *Ferdinand Magellan* for the train trip back to Independence, Missouri. Thousands of people were at the station waiting for them. The crowd called out, "So long, Harry!" and "Good luck, Harry!"

Truman walked back to the rear platform of the train and waved to the cheering crowd, just as he had done years before on his whistle-stop campaign tours. As the train left the station, he smiled and gave a farewell salute. "Everybody in the station started singing 'Auld Lang Syne,'" Margaret Truman recalled. Many were in tears. But not Bess Truman. For her, going home was a dream come true.

CHAPTER THIRTEEN

INDEPENDENCE DAYS

*I am ready to hazard an opinion...that Harry
Truman will eventually win a place as president, if not
as a hero, alongside Jefferson and Theodore Roosevelt.*
—Professor Clinton Rossiter,
Cornell University

The Trumans were deeply moved by the cheering crowd of
five thousand people who came to say good-bye to them in
Washington, D.C. "I'll never forget it if I live to be a hundred," Truman said as he waved good-bye from the train.
Never again, it seemed, would Harry Truman see such a
heartwarming show of support. But when the train arrived
in Independence, more than eight thousand people were
there to welcome them home. Bess Truman was almost
speechless when she saw the huge gathering in her hometown. "This makes it all worth it," she said.

Once settled at home on Delaware Street, the same home
Harry and Bess moved into as newlyweds, Truman continued

The years 1955 and 1956 were pleasantly eventful for Truman, with the publication of his Memoirs *(left) and Margaret's marriage (right).*

his early morning walks, as he had done in Washington, and worked on his *Memoirs.* The first volume, *Year of Decisions,* was published in 1955, and the second, *Years of Trial and Hope,* came out in 1956. *Mr. Citizen* and *Truman Speaks* were published in 1960. Books and family would be Truman's main interests during his retirement.

In 1956 Margaret married Elbert Clifton Daniel Jr., an editor at the *New York Times.* Margaret and Clifton had four children—Clifton, William, Harrison, and Thomas— all of whom provided happy moments for their proud grandparents. They enjoyed family gatherings in New York and Independence and took trips together to Florida.

A "SOURCE OF LIGHT AND REASON"

The biggest public event of Truman's post-presidential years was the opening of the Truman Library, just a few blocks from the Truman home, in 1957. The library, he insisted,

President Truman was proud of the Truman Library and especially fond of the Thomas Hart Benton mural. The library, which opened July 6, 1957, was the first constructed under the 1955 Presidential Libraries Act.

⸺⸺⸺⸺⸺⸺⸺ ◇ ⸺⸺⸺⸺⸺⸺⸺

was to be a vital center for the study of American history and the lives of all the presidents—not just his own. He went to his office in the library almost every day of the week. He loved talking with visitors about the center's historic collection, including the mural "Independence and the Opening of the West" by Thomas Hart Benton that adorned the lobby. This painting depicts the Plains Indians and the migration of the early settlers to Missouri. It also shows the Missouri River landing in the 1840s, when Truman's grandparents docked there. Benton, a Missouri-born artist, was "the best . . . painter in America!" Truman said.

Truman liked to show young people his copy of *Great Men and Famous Women,* the inspiring gift he received from his mother on his tenth birthday. Above all, he loved to talk to them about American history. "To me," he said, "there is nothing more rewarding than to stand before young people and find them so vitally interested in everything pertaining to the affairs of the country and the world."

Memorable occasions continued to highlight Truman's life in the 1960s. In 1961, at a White House dinner given in his honor by President and Mrs. John F. Kennedy, Truman was treated to a special concert in the East Room. After pianist Eugene List completed his program of music by Mozart and Chopin, he asked Truman to play. Truman was "as pleased as a man could possibly be."

In 1965 President Lyndon Johnson went to the Truman Library to sign historic legislation that enacted Medicare. At the ceremony, Johnson called Truman "the real daddy of Medicare." It was Truman who had urged medical coverage for the elderly, years before. The following year, the Harry S. Truman Center for the Advancement of Peace was dedicated at Hebrew University in Jerusalem. "I will be comforted by the hope that this center will become a major source of light and reason toward the achievement of peace," Truman said.

Truman takes a turn at the piano (left) during a 1961 presidential dinner given in his honor. An idea Truman set in motion becomes reality as President Lyndon Johnson signs the 1965 Medicare Act (right).

*The Truman family vacationing
in Florida, 1962*
✧ ————————

During the 1960s, Truman, now in his eighties, had to be hospitalized twice: first after he slipped and fell at home, then during a bout with the flu. Yet he remained active and in good spirits. He pored over the daily newspapers and read books from his vast collection. A reporter once asked him if he liked to read himself to sleep. "No, young man," Truman said firmly. "I like to read myself awake."

Truman grew more frail. In the summer of 1972, he was hospitalized because of severe stomach problems and in December for lung congestion. Bess Truman kept a constant vigil at the hospital. When Margaret was told of his worsening condition, she left New York immediately to be with her mother and father. Harry Truman died at Kansas City's Research Hospital and Medical Center on December 26, 1972. He was eighty-eight years old.

On December 27, after a small family service, his closed casket was placed, as he had requested, in the lobby of the Truman Library, beneath Thomas Hart Benton's mural. An estimated 75,000 people, including President Nixon and former President Lyndon Johnson, passed by the casket that day. The long line of people stretched from the library to the highway beyond it. "The whole town was a friend of Harry's," one man said. Truman was buried in the court-yard of the library the following day.

President Truman was remembered in many languages all over the world. His obituary in the *New York Times* covered seven pages. Even *Time* magazine and the *Wall Street Journal,* which had criticized him in the past, called him "one of the great figures of the century." Among the hundreds of tributes to Truman, one by Adlai Stevenson of Illinois stands out. Truman's life, he said, "was an example of America's ability to yield up, from the most unremarkable origins, the most remarkable men."

As Truman's mother had said decades earlier: "I knew that boy would amount to something from the time he was nine years old. He could plow the straightest row of corn in the county. He could sow wheat so there wasn't a bare spot in the whole field."

President Truman lies in state in 1972.

POSTSCRIPT

Bess Truman died in 1982, ten years after her husband. She was buried next to him in the courtyard of the Truman Library, as both had wished.

Margaret Truman has become a writer of popular mysteries. *Murder in Havana,* the eighteenth book in her Capital Crimes series, was published in 2001. Her books include *Harry S. Truman* (1972), *Women of Courage* (1976), *Letters from Father* (1981), *Bess W. Truman* (1986), *Where the Buck Stops* (1989), and *First Ladies* (1995).

————————————— ✧ —————————————

The gravesites of Harry Truman and Bess Truman are located at the Truman Library in Independence, Missouri.

Bess Truman

Bess Truman treasured her privacy. She enjoyed reading mysteries, going to the movies with Margaret, and taking in baseball games. She hated publicity and repeatedly denied requests for interviews and speeches. On one occasion, however, she agreed to answer a "questionnaire" for reporters, and she did so in her own direct manner:

What qualities did she think would be the greatest asset to the wife of a President?

Good health and a well-developed sense of humor.

Did she think there would ever be a woman President of the United States?

No.

Would she want to be President?

No.

Would she want Margaret to be First Lady?

No.

If it had been left to her own free choice, would she have gone into the White House in the first place?

Most definitely would not have.

What would you like to do and have your husband do when he is no longer President?

Return to Independence.

TIMELINE

1884   Harry S. Truman is born on May 8, in Lamar, Missouri.

1901   Truman graduates from high school. After working for the Santa Fe Railroad, he takes a job at the National Bank of Commerce in Kansas City, Missouri.

1905   Truman joins the National Guard. His father's financial problems force Harry to return to the family farm.

1917   The United States enters World War I.

1918   Truman serves as an artillery captain for the U.S. Army in France.

1919   Truman marries Bess Wallace. They move in with Bess's mother at 219 North Delaware Street in Independence, Missouri. Harry and his friend Eddie Jacobson open a haberdashery, Truman & Jacobson.

1922   Truman & Jacobson closes, leaving Truman with a large amount of debt. Truman is elected to the post of eastern judge for Jackson County, Missouri.

1924   The Trumans' only child, Mary Margaret is born.

1926   Truman is elected presiding judge of Jackson County.

1934   Truman is elected to the U.S. Senate.

1941   After a Japanese surprise attack on Pearl Harbor, the United States enters World War II. Truman presides over the Truman Committee, which investigates defense projects.

1944   Truman is elected vice president on the Roosevelt-Truman ticket.

1945 President Roosevelt dies on April 12. Harry S. Truman becomes president of the United States. Germany surrenders on May 7. Truman authorizes the use of atomic bombs on Japan. Japan surrenders on September 2, ending World War II.

1946 Truman confronts national railroad workers' strike.

1947 Truman becomes the first president of the United States to speak to the National Association for the Advancement of Colored People (NAACP).

1948 Congress passes the Marshall Plan, which will provide billions in aid to European democracies. Truman is the first world leader to recognize the State of Israel. Truman orders the Berlin Airlift. Truman runs for reelection against Thomas Dewey and wins by a narrow margin.

1949 Truman signs the North Atlantic Treaty, making the United States a charter member of NATO.

1950 Communist North Korea invades South Korea. Truman dispatches troops to defend South Korea. Two Puerto Rican men attempt to assassinate Truman.

1951 Truman relieves General Douglas MacArthur as commander of U.S. and UN forces in the Far East.

1952 Truman declines to run for a second full term as president.

1953 After leaving office, Truman and Bess move back to Independence, Missouri.

1957 The Harry S. Truman Library opens in Independence, Missouri.

1972 Truman dies on December 26 at the age of eighty-eight.

SOURCE NOTES

7 Harry S. Truman, *The Wit and Wisdom of Harry S. Truman,* Ralph Keyes, ed. (New York: Harper Collins, 1995), 58.

7 David McCullough, *Truman* (New York: Touchstone/Simon & Schuster, 1992), 341.

8 Ibid., 341–342.

9 Harry S. Truman, *Memoirs,* vol. 1, *Year of Decisions* (Garden City, NY: Doubleday, 1955), 5.

10 Margaret Truman, *Harry S. Truman* (New York: William Morrow, 1972), 209.

11 Arthur Gelb, et al., eds., *The New York Times Great Lives of the Twentieth Century* (New York: Times Books, 1988), 617.

11 Ibid., 615.

11 Ibid., 617.

12 *Weekly Reader: 60 Years of News for Kids, 1928–1988* (New York: World Almanac, 1988), 77.

13 Truman, *Wit and Wisdom,* 41.

16 McCullough, 37.

18 Gelb, et al., 622.

19 Truman, *Wit and Wisdom,* 39.

19 McCullough, 41.

20 Margaret Truman, *Harry S. Truman,* 47.

20 Ibid.

21 Truman, *Memoirs,* vol. 1, 125.

22 McCullough, 44.

23 Ibid., 49.

25 Truman, *Wit and Wisdom,* 34.

28 Cleanth Brooks, et al., eds., *American Literature: The Makers and the Making,* vol. 11 (New York: St. Martin's Press, 1973), 1276.

29 Truman, *Memoirs,* vol. 1, 121.

29 Ibid., 122.

30 W. J. Rolfe, ed., *The Complete Poetical Works of Tennyson* (Boston: Houghton Mifflin, 1898), 550.

32 Truman, *Wit and Wisdom,* 29.

33 McCullough, 67.

33 Ibid.

34 Ibid., 72.

36 Ibid., 73.

37 Ibid., 92.

39 Robert H. Ferrell, ed., *Dear Bess: The Letters From Harry to Bess Truman, 1910–1959* (New York: Norton, 1983), 145.

40 Ibid., 178.

40 Ibid., 186.

41 Truman, *Wit and Wisdom,* 28.

42–43 Truman, *Memoirs,* vol. 1, 129–130.

43 Ferrell, *Dear Bess,* 274.

44–45 Truman, *Memoirs,* vol. 1, 133.

47 McCullough, 166.

47 Ibid., 168.

48 Ibid., 169.

48 Ibid., 170.

48 Ibid., 173–174.

48 Ibid., 174.

48 Ibid.

49 Ibid.

50 Truman, *Wit and Wisdom,* 68.

52 Truman, *Memoirs,* vol. 1, 173.

53 Ibid.

54 Margaret Truman, *Harry S. Truman,* 172.

55 Gelb, et al., 624.

55 Margaret Truman, *Harry S. Truman,* 185–186.

55 Truman, *Memoirs,* vol. 1, 198.

56 "Truman" on *The American Experience,* PBS, 4/30/01.

57 Truman, *Wit and Wisdom,* 124.

58 Margaret Truman, *Harry S. Truman,* 221.

58 Gelb, et al., 615.
58 Margaret Truman, *Harry S. Truman,* 209.
58–59 Ibid., 211.
59 Truman, *Memoirs,* vol. 1, 199.
60 Ferrell, *Dear Bess,* 522.
62 Gelb, et al., 641.
63 "Truman," PBS, 4/30/01.
63 Ibid.
64 Truman, *Wit and Wisdom,* 69.
64 McCullough, 462.
65 Ibid., 463.
66 Gelb, et al., 620.
66 Ferrell, *Dear Bess,* 524.
66 Ibid.
66 Ibid.
70 Margaret Truman, *Letters From Father: The Truman Family's Personal Correspondence* (New York: Arbor House, 1981), 99.
73 Gelb, et al., 637.
74 McCullough, 631.
76 Margaret Truman, *Harry S. Truman,* 221.
77 Ibid., 43.
78 McCullough, 728.
78 Ibid., 729.
79 Ibid., 734.
79 Margaret Truman, *Harry S. Truman,* 401.
80 Ibid., 398.
81 Gelb, et al., 637.
83 Alonzo L. Hamby, *Man of the People: A Life of Harry S. Truman,* (New York: Oxford University Press, 1995), 472.
83 Margaret Truman, *Harry S. Truman,* 3.
84 McCullough, 860.
85 Ibid., 827.
85 Ibid.
85 Ibid., 827–828.
85 Ibid., 828.
85 Margaret Truman, *Harry S. Truman,* 3.

86 McCullough, 829.
87 Hamby, 562.
87 Gelb, et al., 640.
88 Ibid., 630.
89 Ibid., 637.
89 Ibid., 641.
90 "Truman," PBS, 4/30/01.
90 McCullough, 886.
91 Ibid.
91 Ibid., 574.
91 Gelb, et al., 632.
92 Ibid., 640.
92 Ibid.
93 McCullough, 920.
93 Ibid., 922.
93 Margaret Truman, *Harry S. Truman,* 559.
94 Gelb, et al., 640–641.
94 "Truman," PBS, 4/30/01.
96 McCullough, 969.
96 Gelb, et al., 632.
97 McCullough, 975.
97 Gelb, et al., 634.
97 Ibid., 635.
98 McCullough, 986.
99 Ibid., 989.
99 Ibid., 990.
99 Ibid., 992.
99 *Weekly Reader: 60 Years of News for Kids, 1928–1988,* 77.
101 McCullough, 576.

BIBLIOGRAPHY

Acheson, Dean. *Among Friends: Personal Letters of Dean Acheson.* Edited by David S. McClellan and David C. Acheson. New York: Dodd, Mead, 1980.

Bennett, Charles. "Truman, the Bomb, and Today's Peril." *New York Times*, July 5, 1985.

Brooks, Cleanth, R. W. B. Lewis, and Robert Penn Warren, eds., *American Literature: The Makers and the Making.* Volume 1. New York: St. Martin's Press, 1973.

Daniel, Clifton, ed. *Chronicle of the 20th Century.* Mount Kisco, NY: Chronicle Publications, 1987.

Ferrell, Robert H., ed. *Dear Bess: The Letters from Harry to Bess Truman, 1910–1959.* New York: Norton, 1983.

Gelb, Arthur, A. M. Rosenthal, and Marvin Siegel, eds., *The New York Times Great Lives of the Twentieth Century.* New York: Times Books, 1988.

Gordon, Lois, and Alan Gordon. *American Chronicle, Six Decades in American Life, 1920–1980.* New York: Atheneum, 1987.

Hamby, Alonzo, L. *Man of the People: A Life of Harry S. Truman.* New York: Oxford University Press, 1995.

Haynes, Richard F. *The Awesome Power: Harry S. Truman as Commander in Chief.* Baton Rouge, LA: Louisiana State University Press, 1973.

Hersey, John. *Aspects of the Presidency.* New Haven, CT: Ticknor and Fields, 1980.

Marshall, George. *Memoirs of My Services in the World War.* Boston: Houghton Mifflin, 1974.

McCullough, David. *Truman.* New York: Touchstone/Simon & Schuster, 1992.

Roosevelt, Eleanor. *The Autobiography of Eleanor Roosevelt.* New York: DaCapo Press, 1992.

"Truman." *The American Experience.* Written and produced by David Grubin. 4 hours. PBS, April 30, 2001. Television program.

Truman, Harry S. *Memoirs.* Volume 1, *Year of Decisions.* Garden City, NY: Doubleday, 1955.

————. *Memoirs.* Volume 2, *Years of Trial and Hope.* Garden City, NY: Doubleday, 1956.

————. *Mr. Citizen.* New York: Geis Associates, 1960.

————. *Truman Speaks.* New York: Columbia University Press, 1960.

Truman, Margaret. *Harry S. Truman.* New York: William Morrow, 1972.

————. ed. *Letters from Father: The Truman Family's Personal Correspondence.* New York: Arbor House, 1981.

————. ed. *Where the Buck Stops: The Personal and Private Writings of Harry S. Truman.* New York: Warner, 1989.

Truman, Margaret, with Margaret Cousins. *Souvenir: Margaret Truman's Own Story.* New York: McGraw Hill, 1956.

Weekly Reader: 60 Years of News for Kids, 1928–1988. New York: World Almanac, 1988.

FURTHER READING

Coerr, Eleanor. *Sadako and the Thousand Paper Cranes.* New York: Puffin Books, 1999.

Cohen, Daniel. *The Manhattan Project.* Brookfield, CT: Twenty-First Century Books, 1999.

Darby, Jean. *Douglas MacArthur.* Minneapolis: Lerner Publications Company, 1989.

Feinberg, Barbara Silberdick. *Bess Wallace Truman.* New York: Children's Press, 1998.

Harris, Jacqueline L. *History and Achievement of the NAACP.* New York: Franklin Watts, 1992.

Isserman, Maurice. *The Korean War.* New York: Facts on File, 1992.

———. *World War II.* New York: Facts on File, 1991.

La Doux, Rita C. *Missouri.* Minneapolis: Lerner Publications Company, 2002.

Monroe, Judy. *The Rosenberg Cold War Spy Trial: A Headline Court Case.* Berkeley Heights, NJ: Enslow Publishers, 2001.

Morris, Jeffrey. *The Truman Way.* Minneapolis: Lerner Publications Company, 1995.

Raven, Margot Theis. *Mercedes and the Chocolate Pilot: A True Story of the Berlin Airlift and the Candy That Dropped from the Sky.* Chelsea, MI: Sleeping Bear Press, 2002.

Rice, Earle Jr. *The Cold War.* San Diego: Lucent Books, 2000.

Roberts, Jeremy. *Franklin Delano Roosevelt.* Minneapolis: Lerner Publications Company, 2003.

Sherrow, Victoria. *The Making of the Atom Bomb.* San Diego: Lucent Books, 2000.

Stein, Conrad R. *The Korean War Veterans Memorial.* New York: Children's Press, 2002.

Truman, Harry S. *The Wit and Wisdom of Harry S. Truman.* Edited by Ralph Keyes. New York: HarperCollins, 1995.

Whitman, Sylvia. *Children of the World War II Home Front.* Minneapolis: Carolrhoda Books, Inc., 2001.

———. *Uncle Sam Wants You!* Minneapolis: Lerner Publications Company, 1993.

———. V *is for Victory.* Minneapolis: Lerner Publications Company, 1993.

Winget, Mary. *Eleanor Roosevelt.* Minneapolis: Lerner Publications Company, 2001.

Zindel, Paul. *The Gadget.* New York: HarperCollins Juvenile Books, 2001.

INDEX

ABOUT THE AUTHOR

Caroline Lazo has written numerous biographies of men and women whose lives have helped to shape our own. Her works for Lerner Publications include: *F. Scott Fitzgerald: Voice of the Jazz Age; Leonard Bernstein: In Love with Music;* and *Gloria Steinem: Feminist Extraordinaire.* Two of her biographies written for Lerner—*Alice Walker: Freedom Writer* and *Arthur Ashe*—were selected as Notable Social Studies Trade Books for Young People by the National Council for Social Studies.

Ms. Lazo graduated from the University of Minnesota and attended the International School at the University of Oslo, Norway, the home of her paternal ancestors.

PHOTO ACKNOWLEDGMENTS

The photographs and illustrations in this book are used with the permission of: The White House, pp. 1, 7, 13, 19, 25, 32, 41, 50, 57, 64, 73, 81, 89, 94; U.S. Army/Courtesy of the Harry S. Truman Library, pp. 2, 78, 84; National Archives, pp. 6 [W&C 1372], 60 [NWDNS-111-SC-210014], 63 [AEC-52-4421], 65 [W&C 1356], 82 [W&C 1430]; National Park Service Photograph/Courtesy of the Harry S. Truman Library, pp. 8, 11; © Brown Brothers, p. 9; Harry S. Truman Library, pp. 12, 14, 15, 16 (both), 21, 24, 26, 33, 34, 35, 36, 37, 38, 42, 43, 44, 47, 49, 69, 96, 99, 100; D. P. Thompson/Courtesy of the Harry S. Truman Library, p. 17; Library of Congress, pp. 22 [LC-USZ62-20244], 52 [LC-USZ62-16555], 56 [LC-USZ62-101777], 76 [LC-USZ62-94135], 101 [LC-USZ62-25813]; © MPI/Hulton|Archive, p. 27; © Ernest H. Mills/Hulton|Archive, p. 28; Grinter Photo/Courtesy of the Harry S. Truman Library, p. 30; The *Kansas City Star*/Courtesy of the Harry S. Truman Library, p. 51; U.S. Army Signal Corps/Courtesy of the Harry S. Truman Library, p. 53; National Park Service, Abbie Rowe/Courtesy of the Harry S. Truman Library, pp. 59, 72; Los Alamos National Laboratory, p. 63 (inset); © Bettmann/CORBIS, pp. 67, 68, 75, 77 (both), 83, 90, 95 (right), 98; Laura Westlund (map), 79; MacArthur Memorial, p. 87; Gretta Kepton/Courtesy of the Harry S. Truman Library, p. 91; Dwight D. Eisenhower Library, p. 93; Harry Barth/Courtesy of the Harry S. Truman Library, 95 (left); John F. Kennedy Library [ST 251-12-61], p. 97 (left); Lyndon B. Johnson Library, p. 97 (right).

Cover photo: U.S. Army/Courtesy of the Harry S. Truman Library